CW01370497

For everyone who is figuring it out.

Table of thoughts

Introduction   1

A record of the little things   5

    Feeling present   6
    The Chapel   8
    A warm bowl of soup   10
    A List of Happiness   12
    30,000 feet wild thoughts   14
    Contentment   16
    Jumping off a plane   18
    Fear   20
    What it physically feels to be inspired   22
    City & Suburb   24
    Moments I felt the most alive   26
    Waves   28
    A letter to 16-year-old me   30
    One of those days   32
    One of those nights   34

A record of nostalgia   37

    Carousel   38
    Home   40
    Youth   42
    Room   44
    Music   46
    Memories   48
    Memento   50

A record of souls   53

    My guardian angel   54
    Connected by blood   56
    Unconditionally   58
    Sisterhood   60
    We part to reunite   62
    Unforgettable souls   64
    Soon   66
    Sparrow & eagle   68
    Soulmate   70
    "What's your biggest fear?"   72
    Fwd: A letter to friends that I've yet to meet   74

A record of 2 a.m. thoughts   77

    This path   78
    The shape of us   80
    Uniqueness   82
    The trick of never failing   84
    Chasing after something you don't have   86
    Being a 23   88
    Belief or believe   90
    What-ifs   92
    Live like a time-traveler   96
    Memento mori   98

A record of gratitude   101

    Giving thanks   102

Introduction:
How it all came together

I'd have loved to tell you an athlete's tough journey to the Olympics, or a successful businesswoman earning her first coin type of story. But this is none of that. This is just about how this girl who used to write in her bedroom every day, ended up growing into this woman who decided to self-publish a book. It's really not that dramatic, but it's a story I'd like to share.

My mum bought me my first journal when I was six years old. Since then, the habit of documenting my life through words has stuck with me throughout the years. I wrote down my thoughts before bed every day or else I wouldn't be able to fall asleep. The piles of journals I own are physical records of my childhood and teenage years. I wrote about all the drama at school, things I felt frustrated with, or the most random things described in detail, as if this information would somehow be useful to me decades later.

Writing is my way of self-reflection, and journals are like time capsules for my future self. I'd be able to know what happened and what I was thinking today ten years ago. How cool is that? I was so used to writing things that are unfiltered that I never shared my writings because it means unfolding not only my way of expressing, but my way of thinking.

The education system in my home country is very exam-oriented. In school, we're often taught to criticize work instead of appreciating work. It's always "you should correct this part, because you made this mistake," rarely "this part is very creative, good job." We write according to the standards in order to score in exams. Until University, when I started exploring English literature, I found out that we have control over how work is being analyzed. It is alright if people don't understand or hate your work. Literature itself has value to at least the writers themselves; readers just have the privilege to read it.

It took me a long time to accept the imperfection of my writings and not deprecate every bit of what could've been better (and believe me, I'm still trying). At one point, I got obsessed over polishing my writings to a place where it doesn't sound like me anymore. I change my work to impress others instead of writing what feels authentic to me.

I guess there was a turning point in my life that led me to explore my creative writing journey.

I took this creative writing course during my exchange program in Canada. For the first time, I was encouraged to write whatever I want— no guide, no rules, just creative juice. I was given complete creative freedom to let my thoughts flow in words. I must admit that I was not used to it; I only ever do that in my journals. It's so foreign to me to be showing my work to other classmates and getting feedback from it. The writing part wasn't so bad, but showcasing my work to classmates was a bit uncomfortable for me at first. I felt naked. What would they possibly say about my work? I'm not even sure what I'm writing, and they are supposed to know what I mean?

Fortunately, my classmates were very supportive and only gave constructive feedback to help me improve. It's captivating to see what you wrote from a different perspective too. This groupmate interpreted my poem differently from what I intended it to be but her way of seeing it is fascinating. I love the fact that everyone's experience leads them to understand a piece of writing distinctively. I guess that's the beauty of art.

Gradually, I built my confidence in showing people my work. And that's when I started thinking— maybe my writings aren't that bad after all.

At the end of that semester, I went up to the professor and told her how much I liked the course. And she simply said, "keep writing."

I know they're merely two simple words, but they impacted me more than I realized. The course ended, but my journey of writing had just started from thereon.

A few months later, I decided to channel what I took from the course. I created a public space online to share my writings with strangers to overcome my insecurity. If I do it often enough, I would no longer be intimidated by it. And maybe I'd meet some like-minded people along the way.

So that's how I embarked on my writing journey.

I've always wished to publish a book one day, but I thought I'd only do it when I'm "good enough." But at one point, I realized that I'd never reach my own standard. Perhaps it's just an excuse for me to procrastinate after all. So while I still have this passion burning in me, I decided to just go for it.

The writings in this book are not my journal entries, unfortunately (or should I say fortunately because I'm saving you from the cringe). They are pieces that I wrote within the last 4 years, each encapsulating a specific feeling, memory, or life lesson. I hope you can resonate with my writings, see yourself in my words, and feel something.

till she flies again

A record of the little things

Feeling present

I'm now sitting on a bench inside this park, fully taking in all the senses, acknowledging everything around me. The autumn breeze brushes through my hair, bugs flying around the bushes, palm trees overlooking me from above. I hear birds, buses, planes flying by once in a while and passerby's chatter.

Moments like this are when I feel the most present.

I don't remember the last time I just sat outside, not worrying about where to go next and just observing.

It's almost 5 p.m. Parents are taking their children home from school. This girl in school uniform is skipping with a chocolate bar in her hand. When I was just a little girl, that snack after school was the best treat in the world. Getting a pack of cookies after a long school day was the most rewarding thing. Back when the most minuscule things easily fulfilled us. As we grow older, cookies are not valuable enough to satisfy us; cookies became toys; toys became phones. It keeps getting bigger and bigger. Paradoxically, now what gives me the most joy are the simplest things.

I didn't realize I subconsciously avoid interactions with the outside world when I'm alone in a social setting. My eyes are always glued to the phone, ears blasted with music from the earphones. I'm neglecting the scenery and people in this beautiful reality of the dream.

till she flies again

I'm sitting here, taking it all in for a long time, but definitely not the last time.

The Chapel

I stepped into a sacred chapel
In this white snowy morning
The enchanting lullaby echoes
Around the high up ceiling

Soft blaring footsteps
On the odor of ancient wood
The motionless statue
Giving it a tranquil mood

Light shining through
Colorful stained glass
The chandelier outgrew
By the miserable candles

My Heart itched
It whispered a cryptic melody
I left behind
The solitary of my prayer

till she flies again

A warm bowl of soup

She pours a bowl fresh from the pot
aroma filling up the whole room
she goes
"Just what I needed in a cold winter morning."

Lets it sit
tests the heat
with the tips of her fingers
Wraps them around the bowl slowly
to feel the comfort
One sip from her silver spoon
soothing sensation spreads
around her mouth into her stomach
the aftertaste is even sweeter

She wants to save this soup
forever if she could
but time will only take its moment away
Maybe she could take a picture
to reminisce it later
but nothing compares
even if the heat might burn her tongue
if she is mistaken

till she flies again

Lost in her thoughts
steam runs low
seize it while it lasts
It's time
She reaches the bottom of the bowl
indulging in the last bit
until it's gone

She'd do it again
but things come to an end
the only thing different is that
the warmth runs through her blood
and set her off to a new day

till she flies again

A List of Happiness

- intimate heart-to-heart talk
- long letters
- my parents' food
- tight hugs
- the smell of parchment
- a copy of my friend's favorite book
- bath & music
- clear blue sky
- fresh clean bedsheet
- fairy lights + candle + pen + diary
- silly pictures and videos in my photo album
- a surprise package in the mailbox

till she flies again

30,000 feet wild thoughts

We're flying at an altitude of 30,000 feet, and I feel like writing something.

To me, flying is a therapeutic activity. I never saw it as merely a prerequisite for a journey; it's part of the journey. It's alone time, with no internet distraction, just me, the sky, and probably some music blasting in my ears. I like sitting beside the window, indulging myself deep in my thoughts while admiring the marshmallow sea in the thin air. It's also when existential questions start surfacing in my brain.

The sky makes me ponder, makes me miss places, miss people. It is the only thing that looks the same wherever I am. When I feel homesick in a foreign country, looking up at this blue canvas brings me home; When I miss people, I see them inside those fluffy clouds; When I am distressed, it reminds me of how big the world is and how trivial my problems are.

Flying is a miracle in its nature. I can't begin to imagine how much determination it took the Wright brothers to go after this seemingly impossible vision. The failures that came with all the attempts they had made to fly. Imagine telling the world that you were inventing a machine that would give humans wings. How many people would be teasing them behind their back for this bizarre idea? I guess we are so used to flying that we sometimes forget how magnificently incredible it is.

It also reminds me of how lucky we are to live in a time where we can connect with people who live in the opposite

till she flies again

part of the world. When we have access to almost anywhere in the world; when distance is no longer a boundary.
The magic of the sky— again, I let my thoughts wander around those clouds.

Contentment

Do you ever just get this sudden wave of contentment in the most unexpected times?

You could be standing alone in a packed bus, lying in bed struggling to fall asleep, waiting in line for the metro to arrive. It just comes so naturally. It feels so chemical— this rush of gratefulness that you feel about people in your life, and experiences you've encountered. You feel your eyes welling up, the corner of your mouth curving up. You try to fight them, but your cheek just can't stop lifting. You don't care what people would think if they saw your face. At this moment, you just feel fully content.

till she flies again

Jumping off a plane

It was a chilly morning. I had to wake up before sunrise to prepare myself for the jump. The skydive shuttle picked me up from the apartment at around 7 a.m. On my ride there, I was feeling surprisingly calm. I guess the fact that I was going to jump off a plane hadn't quite sunk in yet. A few other first-time skydivers were on the shuttle, so it was comforting to know that I wasn't doing it all alone.

It was about an hour before the jump, but luckily I met a new friend to divert my mind from worrying. So, after a bit of a hustle, we were back on that shuttle and it took us to the airport, where we would take the aircraft.

I was paired with an instructor who my life would be depended on (literally). He probably got asked this question a lot, but I asked it anyway, "how many times have you jumped before?" and of course, he had to tell me that it's his first time to freak me out even more.

When the aircraft took off, I didn't feel much inside. I had a quick prep talk to myself inside my head. Ok, this really is happening.

Panic started to kick in when the first skydiver opened the aircraft door. I felt the wind rushing in, and the tension began to build up. Knowing that I was the second one to take the leap, I tried to settle the unease that's accumulating inside me. Then, I witnessed the skydivers jump off and disappear out of sight like the wind.

till she flies again

Soon later I was nudged to the edge of the plane by my instructor. I had a split second to look out upon mother earth before leaning my head back. It's the most beautiful sight I'd ever beholden. After that, my mind went blank for a moment. The instructor did a little push, and we were out of the plane.

The first few seconds were a blur since my senses were overloaded. At 120mph, the strong wind brushed through my face, and the rush of air made such a loud noise, yet I felt utterly peaceful. It didn't feel like falling at all. It felt like floating, more precisely, flying. I couldn't contain my excitement and kept screaming, "I'm flying!". This is what flying feels like; this is the state of total freedom.

After about 45 seconds of freefall, my instructor launched the parachute and glided to the beach. Those few minutes were when I could fully capture everything that's beneath me— the clear coastline, tiny houses, moving cars, and long road. My mind was serene as the wind took us back to the landing zone.

Fear

I went ship jumping for the first time the other day.

I'm not particularly scared of height, but the idea of falling from a ship is still intimidating.

Standing on the edge of the boat, I looked at the depth beneath me. The coach patted me on the back, hinting at me to jump. I held on to my safety jacket and started to panic—wait, what do I do again? Do I just keep my legs straight the whole time or? What if I drown?

"Go, girl, go," I told myself. I don't know where that gut came from.

I surrendered my body to gravity and got sucked into this black hole. I was already soaked in saltwater before I could register what just happened. The aching thighs from slapping on the water surface, a pair of flushing hands, and red eyes—yet all these didn't matter because the only thing I was thinking was, wow, I did it.

We did 9 more jumps after the first try, each being more challenging than the previous one. You might think I would have gotten used to it on my 10th jump, but no, it didn't get any less scary each time. Every time the coach told us we were stepping it up, I doubted myself if I could do it. I had even considered chickening out by lying to the coach that I was sick. But I did all the 10 jumps at last. I thought that a 2.5 metre jump was my limit, but the coach kept pushing and pushing the "limit". I'd proven myself wrong every time.

I realised I set limits for myself because I don't believe that I could've achieved more. I hold myself back from trying and this has hindered me from many unforeseen possibilities. Conquering fear is probably the only way to achieving more great things in life. Everything seems impossible until it's been done. We just need that little push to discover the version of us that is capable of achieving a lot more.

Do more things that you are afraid of so you'd no longer be afraid.

What it physically feels to be inspired

There's this feeling when a rush of serotonin goes through your body. It moves the waves of the ocean inside you, overflowing. Your brain starts shooting confetti which has gotten too fast for you to clean up. You feel this warmth around your throat, and your heartbeat is beating more quickly than usual. You're so deep in your thoughts that you almost lose the rhythm of your breath.

That match inside you lights up and catches fire. You feel like running; you feel like telling everyone about this. This excitement of wanting to create something you'd be proud of, and that you want people to appreciate too.

Share it with people before the flame dies down again. For you know that inspiration is a butterfly flying aimlessly around you, it's hard to catch. And when you do seize it, study it, and embrace it.

till she flies again

City & Suburb

One summer, I visited my old roommate in a small town and stayed with her family for a few days. For the first time in a while, I was out in an isolated area away from the city. It felt weird surrounded by a green field but not crowds; looking up to a wide sky but not tall buildings. I was in awe to see trees from miles away and thousands of bright stars at night.

My friend and I went kayaking in a lake in the neighborhood. In the middle of it, I stopped, and just took everything in. The sun was strong but shining on my skin gently, the fluffy clouds looked so close to the ground as if I could reach them with my hands, the waves were pushing my kayak backwards. I rested my hands in the water to cool myself down a little. I looked at the trees on the shore from far away and giggled to myself how my friend said it's just a "small lake". I caught a glimpse of some large grey stones. Oh, it's a graveyard. I looked away to the other side and saw some kids playing at the beach. I think they're looking in my direction. Are they really? I squinted my eyes. I think they're waving at me now.

I got carried away by my thoughts. At that moment, all my worries went away. I felt alive.

A fast-paced city makes me feel like I'm just living from day to day. I just exist, have fun, and do it again. It gave me clarity after allowing myself to take a step back, slow down, and let my mind wander.

The community feels so much tighter in the suburb. Everyone knows one another, and helps whenever anyone

till she flies again

needs it. They say hi to each other on the street and ask how their day is going. They communicate through regular morning breakfast meet-ups and phone calls instead of text messages. Isn't it ironic how I live in such a dense city where people's distance is so close, yet their relationships are so distant? I can't even recognize my neighbors living on my floor.

I sat next to my friend in the driver's seat, taking me to a nearby village. If you could choose, I asked her, would you live in the big city or the suburb? She said, "I used to fantasize about living in the big city before visiting. I guess everyone does. The city seems so much more exciting. But when I experienced living there, I realized it's not really for me. So, the suburb, Angel, I would choose the suburb."

We sat in the car in silence. I thought to myself what my answer would be.

Moments I felt the most alive

- Exchanging thoughts with someone special at 1am
- Looking up at the big blue sky in the middle of a lake
- Instantly connecting with someone I met for the first time
- Catching up with an old friend about all the things I've missed
- Laughing about high school memories with friends on the staircase in a mall
- Seeing my parents hold onto each other like it's their first date
- Jumping to songs in a concert
- Driving four-wheelers in a big empty backyard at full speed
- Watching and listening to sea waves hit the shore during sunset
- Getting on a bus that I don't know the destination to
- Singing and dancing to my favorite playlist alone in the bedroom

till she flies again

till she flies again

Waves

Arching bones want nothing
but to rip that brain off of your body
Detaching from
the utter misery

Hands
but nothing to grasp at
Feet
but nowhere to walk to
Holding onto
the last piece of hope
dragging it along
as you crash into the deep ocean

Swallowed by the nature of life
Big waves wash over you
Tides keep coming
You let your weight sink
but
not giving it power to kill you
Till it's unbearable
Pull string
Glide to the surface again

Remember this sensation
Right here
And when you're up flying again
Wings will feel lighter
As you left all the salt with the ocean

till she flies again

A letter to 16-year-old me

I found a letter at the back of my old journal, one that I wrote to my future self when I was 16. I vaguely remember writing a letter like this, and I couldn't wait for my future self, aka me, to read it.

I thought I'd cry or get emotional reading it but I guess my words weren't that tears triggering. If anything, they gave me the giggle instead. In a lot of ways, I still think like my old self— I'm curious about the future; I still feel unsure about directions in life; but I've definitely experienced and learned so much more than her. What worried me back then seems so trivial now.

You told me that you wanted me to write a letter back to you, so here it is, my 16-year-old self:

Hey,

I'm glad you wrote to me. It's nice getting a letter from you.

First of all, I just wanna let you know that all went well with your biology report and 450-word Model United Nations essay. So don't stress too much about it ok.

I know you have many wonders about what your future will look like, so I won't spoil it for you. But just know that a majority of what you envisioned has come true. You've worked hard to get to where you wanted to be. And I thank you for all the sweat and tears that you've put in so I can have this life right here. I assure you that your hard work will pay off.

The fam's been doing well btw. We've been the tightest than ever. Can you believe how much your sister has grown tho? She is almost getting into University now. Isn't it crazy? She is just a little kid over on your side.

Your letter did appear in the perfect timing actually. I'm in a place where I'm feeling a bit frustrated with things I don't have control over. So it's a perfect pick-me-up. Reading your letter reminds me of how much the current time isn't really that crucial as I make it seem. What you thought mattered a lot back then is so irrelevant to me now. Perhaps now I shouldn't stress so much about what's on my mind because I already know what my future self will say. So, thanks for this. You have no idea how much impact this letter you decided to write because you were bored has made.

My sleeping schedule has been kinda a mess lately but I'm learning to take better care of myself, don't worry.

I hope these are what you wanted to know. Believe in yourself. You are doing just fine.

Sincerely,
You, 9 years later

One of those days

the sun whispers
to my freckles
morning eyes battle
two magnets with different poles

empty stomach yet sick of
the thoughts of breakfast
clutch onto my three pillows
never want to let go

stare at the ceiling thinking
why I slept at four a.m.
a rush of regret knowing
tonight I'd do it all over again

reach for my phone first thing
airplane mode off
five ding dings
cloudy brain blows away the fog

to-dos rehearsed themselves
in my head yet my body
still soaked in the comfort
of my bedsheets

coming at the sixth times
of alarm snoozes
knowing for a fact
that there'd be a seventh

till she flies again

dreaming about the luxury
when I got eight hours of sleep
somehow tiredness still creeps
out of my bare skin

inhale, exhale, inhale, exhale
nine breaths in
energy flowing from
my hair to my nails

ready to leave this fluff
give myself ten more seconds
now read this poem over
and count with me again

One of those nights

2:50 a.m
Why does the moon feel extra bright
Room peculiarly noisy tonight

Everything distracts me as I open my eyes
Siren starts ringing in my mind as I shut them tight
Scenes keep flashing
How do I make them stop
I wish there's a button
Just to turn it off

Roll my body from side to side
Bedsheet doesn't seem to hold me right
Organs feel out of place
Hair doesn't sit well on my face

Try sitting up
Stretch my body a little
Pull myself back to the mattress
And mind again starts to whistle

Clock clicking knowing
I'm going to blame myself in the morning
But how do I get out of this
Kindly, brain, please,
Just let me sleep.

till she flies again

till she flies again

till she flies again

A record of nostalgia

Carousel

Take a train to an unknown destination;
let out all your frustration.
Unclear of where it will lead you,
the only thing sealed is it'd be somewhere new.

Once you board the train,
empty suitcase, hollow, hollow brain,
you are devoted to this thing called life—
an adventure that now you can call mine.
Passengers, your company,
amidst friends, partner, and family.
Rediscover yourself in this unanticipated journey
when self-doubt is your only enemy.

With ongoing scenery outside the window,
are you a sailor hovering with sea wave;
or an astronaut floating pointlessly in space?
So whenever you stray,
remember the place you stay
for life is merely a carousel after all
drifting back to where you belong.

till she flies again

Home

When I was little, home was just a place to me— this tiny apartment situated between the police office and fire station, next to the mountain. I guess that mentality was developed from the fact that my family had never moved before. I didn't understand the concept of "home".

Reaching adulthood, I had a taste of living outside of this "home". I slowly realized that the concept of home is not a place, but a feeling, of belonging, security, and attachment.

My family and friends make me feel at home. My comfort is built through spending time with them. I became aware that they can't be physically here all the time as our paths take us to different places. So, I developed this shelter within me.

Whenever I start getting attached to a place, I always ask myself— is it the place itself or the people? The answer is always the latter. So whether I've found a place that I feel like I belong to does not matter anymore. What truly matters is, the people are always here, somewhere inside the left side of my chest.

till she flies again

Youth

There are stacks of photo albums in the house that my parents kept even before I was born. These photos were taken at a time when photography was the primary way of capturing moments, and you had to wait for your film to develop to see those photos. It felt surreal looking at pictures of my parents when they were just around my age— free from real adult problems, posing like teenagers, in retro clothes that surprisingly become trendy again 30 years later.

When you grow up seeing your parents as just "your parents", it's easy to forget that they were once our age who also felt lost about their future, who had to figure life out just like us.

Looking at these photos in my hands was like diving into my parents' life journey. It's an evidence of how it all started. There are many questions I want to ask this cute couple in the photos. I wonder how they would feel if I told them what their future would look like in 30 years. And isn't it fascinating that how we, at this point in time, are going to be history someday too? One day, perhaps my children would be wondering the same thing. I wonder what they'd be telling me.

till she flies again

Room

Growing up, I had always dreamed of having a room of my own.

I shared a bedroom with my younger sister for most of my childhood and teenage years. We shared a bunk bed and had very different sleeping schedules. She was always the one who went to bed first while I kept the light on and watched Youtube videos till 2 a.m. But she didn't mind; she was used to it.

My sister got older and no longer fit in her bed, so my dad said perhaps it's finally time to get rid of this bed set. I didn't say anything, but deep down, I wanted to cling on to it a bit longer. I'm very attached to things that feel special to me. The bed was filled with stickers I stuck on when I was little. They're ugly, but every sticker tells a story. I knew I had to say goodbye to it now or later, but I just didn't want to admit it.

I moved to a new room and it was thrilling. I could finally decorate it like how I'd always wanted to; I watched room tour videos to get inspiration; I knew the exact bedsheet I was going to get. I had this vision of how I wanted my room to look. And it is precisely that.

My sister stayed in the old room, and every piece of furniture was kept untouched. I liked that I was having a new space and keeping the childhood room exactly as it was.

A week later, we came back home to something unexpected. Knowing that my sister wanted to get rid of the bunk bed so

till she flies again

badly, my dad secretly revamped the whole room. For the first time, I saw a room without a bunk bed.

It finally struck me that this is not my room anymore, that the childhood room I spent 20 years in was gone. It'd never feel the same.

I went back to my new room and laid on my bed. I pictured everything in my old room, reliving the moments when my mum read me bedtime stories; when I couldn't fall asleep and looked at the stickers in the dark; when I woke up to music blasting from the CD player…

I said goodbye to all these things that'd gone too quickly for me to say farewell to in person. Every corner of the room, I'd remember it just the way it was.

Music

Music has this magical power of encapsulating a feeling, evoking memories in your brain that you have forgotten, in ways that even words cannot do.

Those particular melody and rhythm bring me back to the sensations of that very winter night when I had this song playing in my earphones while hopping off the shuttle bus after a night class. I slowly trembled back to the dorm in my snow boots while breathing inside my scarf, avoiding to inhale the cold chilly air. I could almost hear the crunching sound my boots made when I stepped on the melting snow.

I remember listening to it in bed, struggling to fall asleep at 2 a.m; I remember repeatedly blasting it out of my earphones on the bus, feeling extremely lively; I remember clicking the repeat button because I didn't feel like listening to anything else. It just felt right.

I love listening to a song over and over again to keep the memory alive. Still, contradictorily, when a song stores profound meanings, a special value to me, I almost don't want to listen to it because what if I "ruin" the song by associating it with a new memory? I wouldn't be able to revisit that old memory.

I wonder if it'd still feel the same, if I listen to that song or that playlist 50 years later. Would those sensations still be as vivid? Maybe I would've forgotten about this song, but somehow it would come on shuffle and awake an archive in my brain. Perhaps it's the closest thing to time-traveling.

till she flies again

Memories

My memory isn't the best, but my brain tends to recollect specific scenes distinctively in detail. Sometimes even people around me are surprised that I remember what exactly they did or said a long time ago. But I realized that those memories are often moments that I cherish a lot, even though they might feel like the most random things to remember.

I see myself back to that corridor in school residence on my first day. The anxiety I felt when I didn't know anyone. The sweat on my palm when I first opened my dorm door with two big suitcases resting beside me. The curiosity towards everything around me while I explored this new place. The nerve that suddenly came to me when I laid in bed and realized, damn, I'm staying here for the coming four months.

I remember exactly how I shredded happy tears and jumped up and down in my room after making my first friend in this new environment; exactly how I started a conversation with that person who sat opposite me on the cafeteria table, and I had no idea that this person would become one of the most significant people in my life.

People and things change. That's why memory is the most precious thing. It stays with you always, and no one could ever take it away. I like turning memories into physical forms— photos, videos, or words. If I ever lose my memory one day, they would be a reminder of what a life I had lived. But the most beautiful form of memory will always be the one that lives inside me. It belongs only to me and can only be felt along with my heart.

till she flies again

Memento

That tin box under the shelf is something I find myself going back to when nostalgia hits.

It's a memory box where I store my treasured possessions. Some are more recent, like notes from friends, flight tickets, concert tickets; some are from my childhood, like small toys, bookmarks I got from my primary school teacher, name stamp from kindergarten...

Some are even from before I was born. How is that possible, you might ask.

My mum kept this calendar card of my birth year and my hospital wristband when I was born. One day she even gave me her pregnancy test, but I decided to let her keep it. It's funny because I realized that those two lines are my first-ever appearance in this world. It's such a weird feeling holding that in my hand.

Every item in the box tells a story.

It was one of those nights and I pondered on every item and got lost in my thoughts as I went through everything in the box.

I stumbled upon this letter from my mum that she wrote me when I turned 15. It makes sense how much I like expressing my emotions through writings. It's definitely in the gene.

till she flies again

In the letter, she told the story of her giving birth to me 15 years ago. And oh, how much I sobbed just by reading a couple of lines.

I almost didn't make it, she said. When she went into labor, the navel string wrapped around my neck, and I went through a critical period. I've heard about this story before, but something about reading it just makes it so much more real. We all take "being born" for granted, don't we? As cheesy as it sounds, it's easy to forget that everyone is a miracle from the day they were born.

These tangible memories are my reminders. Whenever I'm lost, I look at them and remind myself where I came from and how I got here. Looking back on the past somehow gives me motivation to push forward. I need that once in a while.

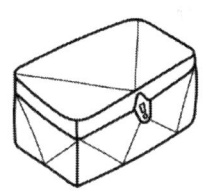

till she flies again

till she flies again

A record of souls

My guardian angel

In the nine years of my life that I was fortunate enough to have him by my side, he always smiled big.

His laughter was contagious, and he walked around with this navy blue umbrella as his cane. He taught me how to hold chopsticks properly and made sure that I was well-fed with the most delicious food. He spoiled me so much that my parents would try to stop him, even though it didn't work 90% of the time. Not being the most verbally expressive, he showed his love through actions, but I could feel it wholeheartedly just the same.

During my summer holiday in kindergarten, he insisted on coming all the way from the south to the north side of the city to visit me every morning. It's around two and a half hours of traveling back and forth. I can't recall a whole lot about that period of my childhood, but I do remember him just sitting on the ground, playing Barbies with me, and listening to me ramble.

In recent years, my parents told me stories in my childhood and I found out that one time I threw a tantrum at him. I stopped him from entering our apartment door by pushing him away, so he had to return home afterward. It still breaks my heart every time I think about this, even though I was probably too young at the time to understand what I'd done.

One of my favorite memories is the time he took me out to the mall and bought me a hello kitty badge maker, a toy that I had dreamed of owning. I was super anxious that my parents would find out that he "had done it" again. It's not like my parents didn't want him to get me anything; It's just that they want me to earn my reward by being a behaved kid instead of handing me gifts directly. Thinking back, it wasn't that big a deal after all, but at that time, the innocent me felt it was the kindest thing anyone could've done for me. I thought to myself, "wow, he took the risk for me again. He is my hero."

In his later years, it's our family's weekly plan to visit him on Saturdays. I remember sitting by his bed when he was lying down sick. In his gentle voice, he told me all these things about how important it is to be a good person in life. I kept nodding and didn't say a word, partly because I didn't want him to notice the tears in my eyes, partly because I knew that I would start sobbing if I spoke anything.

I still think about him a lot.

People around me sometimes say that they consider me a lucky person, who seems to meet good people and encounter miracles. To me, that's not luck. I know that a guardian angel is watching over me, guiding me the way and making my path. And, it's him.

Thank you, grandpa. I hope I make you proud.

Connected by blood

I had no name
Two were one
There was no me
Just us

25 years of knowing her from
Full trust to skeptics
Annoyance to realization
An authority to a friend

Times when I saw her
As a pot of boiling water
Overflows if you turn up
Gets burn if you touch

Times when she picked me up
Though she fell even deeper
Handing me band-aids
When she needed them the most

Unmovable like mountains
She sees light and faith
Trees built up again
Stronger than ever she's made

till she flies again

Times when I noticed her qualities
I see myself in her
Two became one again
Connected evermore

Even after I was born
I never left her
If not in locations
Always in minds

Unconditionally

He never really asked me why I felt sad but
he bought me my favorite ice cream to cheer me up.

He never really liked eating fish head but
he told us he did to save the best part of the fish for us.

He never really asked me about my new job but
he secretly downloaded the app of my company to learn more about it himself.

He never really congratulated me on my graduation but
he found time to come to my graduation photo day even when he was busy.

He never really called me when I travelled alone but
he got so worried about me that he struggled to fall asleep.

He never really showed me his excitement to see me back home but
he cleaned up my room to prepare for my return.

He never really told me how he feels but
I can tell just by looking at him.

I've never really heard him say it out loud but
all these tell me that he loves me more than I know.

till she flies again

Sisterhood

I am aware that time flies by quicker than we can notice. This moment right here will become the past soon. There were moments in life where I wished I had the superpower to slow down time. Because I know that with time, things won't stay the same. Even if I try hard to grasp, it will still slip away.

Watching my sister grow up is the most apparent proof of how fast time passes.

I remember writing this thought in my journal when she was six years old. I had just spent a few days with her and my grandma while my parents were away for a trip. I felt more connected with my sister after spending more one-on-one time with her. Being eight years apart, I had always tried to take up the role of authority when my parents were not here. I'd be the big sister to make sure that she was behaving well and sometimes I missed opportunities to know her deeper.

My mind was clouded with thoughts of my sister getting older. One day, she wouldn't be this adorable bubbly kid who follows me around, copies everything I do, and calls for me in a baby voice. One day, I would wake up not knowing that it's the last day she'd ever let me poke her chubby cheeks and carry her around.

I stopped writing and looked away from my journal. My sister was sleeping peacefully with her soft toys on the bottom bunk. I tried to take in the moment, and captured this scene like a photo in my mind. I told myself that I'd spend more time with her but deep down I knew there was no way to cheat. Time stays the same, no matter how much we want more.

With no surprise, eventually my thoughts back then became the reality. Except, it really wasn't as scary as I thought. I guess that little cute baby sister would never be quite the same, but now I have a lifelong best friend who I can count on for this long ride. I'm excited to see what a persistent and grounded person she will continue to be.

We part to reunite

Have you ever looked forward to something so much that you almost don't want that day to come? Because when it does, it will have to end.

One of my best friends is flying over to visit for the holiday. It's been almost two years since we've seen each other. Though we text nearly every day and have video calls frequently, I still miss her like crazy. It brings tears to my eyes just rehearsing the reunion in my head. But it's not the only thing I rehearse. I also can't help but think about the ending. It'd be like that night all over again.

26th May 2017
10:14 p.m.
We sat across from each other inside a cafe on St Catherine street. Knowing that it'd be the last time we see each other in a while, we just chatted as usual. Just like the first time we met, we talked about anything and everything. It's honestly crazy how I'd only known her for four months, but it felt like I'd known her since forever. She added to my thoughts like they're hers and finished my sentences when I couldn't find the right words.

12:03 a.m.
I looked at my phone and realized that it's almost time for us to catch the last metro back home. I gazed at her, she knew it too. Suddenly we were both silent. I started reaching for the napkin because I felt my eyes welling up. My chest began to ache, and it's coming up to my throat. Words were overflowing, so were the tears. She looked at me and kept shaking her head. "No, no, no, you're gonna come back, and

we'll see each other again very soon." But the flood wasn't stopping. "I have never had to say goodbye like this before." She said in her brittle voice. We wiped our tears and laughed about how ridiculous it was that two girls were weeping inside a cafe. But we didn't care. "It's ok to cry at midnight."

I've looked forward to this day since that night, and I still can't believe we're meeting again in 2 days. I'm feeling both excited and anxious, but mostly excited. I guess the joy of seeing her again has exceeded the pain of parting, if that's even possible.

We part to reunite. I guess it's our thing now.

Unforgettable souls

At different points in life, there are people you encounter that change you as a person. Once you meet them, you carry a piece of them with you onto your ride. They could be friends you met in school who are now your best friends; teachers that later became your life mentors; but could also be that one person you met in summer camp but already forgot the name of, or even that old lady who started having a short conversation with you on the bus.

It's something they did or said, that set you off to a different path of life.

They don't know this— but at that very moment, you put that piece of memory into your life archive, and look back at it as a reminder when you need it.

Who are you thinking of now?

_____

till she flies again

Soon

Sometimes you meet someone for the last time in your life without knowing it. "Bye, see you soon." But tomorrow is not promised. Maybe you will cross paths again, or perhaps you won't, for all the unknowns the future holds.

This is why parting is always hard for me, especially when you are geographically separated. Indeed you say you will meet again soon. But deep down, you know that "soon" is only a word to give yourself hope; it always has been.

Nevertheless, I'm always going to say it because if I believe in it strongly enough, the universe will hear it, and "soon" will become reality. I don't know when, but soon, a reunion will happen.

till she flies again

Sparrow & eagle

Glides, hovers, flutters
In the blue canvas with white splatters
Gladdened by the boundlessness
Such ambiguity to behold

In search of something unknown
Little Sparrow free flows
To a place
Where she can feel at home

A deserted island with no bustle
Unfamiliar chirps and whirs
Trapped echo amid the lofty trees
Her voice lost in the noise

Circling with the flocks
To feel included
Is this the place she desires
Sailing around for answers

A few pairs of wings fallen
Waving to farewell
Once again,
She finds herself flying alone

Alights to rest her wings
An intriguing jungle, she thinks
Monkeys, bears, squirrels
More and more to unravel

till she flies again

An eagle perches
Faithful, driven, and versatile
Foreign yet familiar like families
Dark yet colorful like a kaleidoscope

Exchanging love, thoughts, and passions
Time spent tastes like a vanilla cupcake
Two souls collide into one
She feels at home

Next destination?
Both mutter without answers
Take off where the wind blows
With unplanned plans

Soulmate

— is a term that she thought she knew what it stood for. There were times that she's called someone a soulmate or been called one. She thought, that's it. Until they crossed paths, and that changed the meaning for her.

It's strange. It's like the universe is doing the work for them, and they don't even have to try. There were many occasions that she thought to herself just how crazy it is that this person just speaks her mind, further elaborates her thoughts like it's his. She still remembers how thrilled she was when he first told her that he thinks they are soulmates. It's the first time that she truly felt this word so profoundly. At first, it worried her that they couldn't live up to what it means. Little did she know that they began creating new meanings for this word from that point.

She googled the definition of Soulmate— "a person ideally suited to another as a close friend or romantic partner." She thinks it doesn't fully encapsulate what it really is.

Soulmate, is someone who makes you feel like time stops when you talk to them; someone who stays up talking to you even if it's 4 a.m.; someone who would fly 18 hours just to see you; someone who exchanges feelings with you only by looking into their eyes; someone who teaches you your worth; someone who is as excited as you to figure out what life is together; it's also someone that even if you feel like the world is against you two, you'd still choose to be together.

It's all of the above and so much more.

till she flies again

"What's your biggest fear?"

He asked her.
It's a big question, she thought to herself. She had a quick think.
"Losing someone I love."
It's simply that.
"How about you?" She asked.
Without hesitation, he answered "being forgotten and leaving no trace behind in this world."

She didn't tell him, but from that day on, it became her promise to make sure he never has to face that.

till she flies again

Fwd: A letter to friends that I've yet to meet

Hi friend,

Nice to meet you! I'm not sure if it's too early or too late for me to say that because I don't know you yet, but by the time you read this, we're already a part of each other's lives. I wonder how we met— did we meet at work? At a cafe? What time was it? What were we doing?

I wonder what you're doing right now as I'm writing this. Maybe you live 10,000 miles away, in a different country, but somehow we ended up in the same place at the same time. The universe is still working its way to intertwine our lives. Or maybe we're living in the same neighborhood, but we have yet to acknowledge each other's existence. Either way, know that I'm very excited to meet you. Perhaps you've already left a significant mark in my life, and I couldn't imagine a life without you. Isn't it crazy that now I don't even know what I'm missing out on? How's life before we met, and how's life after?

Well, I guess I can tell you how life was before we met— I have some very lovely people in my life. Some eventually became just acquaintances, but I'm grateful for their company in a specific chapter of my life; Some stick with me through the highs and lows and are always here when I need them. It doesn't matter whether I've known them for 10 years, or 3 months, the right people always stay. I hope you are one of those people. I hope we go on crazy road trips together, talk about our feelings at 3 a.m., and make memories that we'd never forget.

till she flies again

Who knows at what point in our lives we will cross paths, perhaps in a month, or even 30 years from now. Maybe it'd be a time when we least expect it, or a time when we need people around the most. I can go on and on forever with all the possibilities, but we'd only find out when it happens. To you whom I've yet to meet, I can't wait to get to know you, can't wait to hear all the stories that I've been missing out on.

Till the day we meet.

till she flies again

till she flies again

A record of 2 a.m. thoughts

This path

I told myself that I just haven't gotten used to this yet. When I do, it'll all make sense. I waited, waited, and waited.

Or maybe I've already gotten used to it. Perhaps this feeling of uncertainty is just something I have to live with.

I read a quote online, and it goes, "the older you get, the more you realize that no one actually knows what they are doing. Everyone is just pretending."

When I was little, it seemed so clear to me what success was. Success, was getting into University, graduating, and getting a high-paid job. This concept of success was ingrained in my mind because of social expectations. So I followed it and thought that it's all I wanted.

We are pressured to make critical life choices at specific times of life. It's as if we are supposed to know exactly what we want at that moment, no matter they are the electives we have to choose at school, our University selections, or our first jobs.

You reached this intersection that would lead you to different paths. You didn't know which route to take, but the long queue behind you kept pushing, so you had to keep walking. You chose this route that you didn't know if it's for you. You kept strolling for a few years. It didn't feel that bad. There were obstacles along the way, but you powered them all through until you arrived in this swan lake. You did it. Everyone was cheering for you.

till she flies again

But at this point, you'd had enough time to learn about yourself to figure out which path you wanted. It's not the swan lake but the snowy mountain. Yet, you didn't want to come to terms with the fact that you had "wasted" so much time and effort building this path of your own. Look at this glamorous swan, look at everyone cheering for you, you said to yourself, "maybe it's better left this way." So you pretended, pretended that it's what you'd always wanted.

You stayed in the lake for the rest of your life. You never got to the mountain and would never know what beautiful creatures you would find there.

The shape of us

We're constantly spoon-fed with information, chasing after this ever-changing ideal way of living. Sometimes, it feels like we're living for someone else, becoming the person society wants us to be.

When I traveled out of the big city, it was refreshing to remove myself from the noise and distraction. Seeing how suburban people live makes me reflect on the way we city people do. It's like I stepped out of my life a little and look at it from an outsider's point of view. All these norms I'm so used to start to surface, and I ask myself why we do what we do.

I didn't realize how much the surrounding is shaping us as an individual. In a dense city, we search for groups that we feel we belong. The last thing we want to happen is to be considered an outcast, so we try hard to fit in. Subconsciously, we are doing all these things to be included, for it checking our phones on the metro because everyone else is doing it or flaunting the glamorous side of our life on social media. Slowly, the colors of our shirts are the same as everyone else's; our voices are the same as everyone else's; we are considered one of them.

That, however, also means that we are easily pulled away from trying new things. We don't want to be different, to stand out, because it's a form of outcast too. Having a different opinion scares us because we don't want to go against the grain and be judged, so we just do whatever the majority is doing, think like the way the majority is thinking.

till she flies again

In a culture where uniqueness is not celebrated, it's so easy to get caught up in the river's current. Just letting it take you to where it wants you to be.

Uniqueness

Living in an era of social media
a generation that is fed by competitions
Superiority as a metric of self-worth
It's easy to get caught up
in an eternal loop of comparison
Look at this, look at that
Their life seems flawless, carefree, and dreamy
One that everyone strives for
Sorry to spoil it for you
But what you've always been endeavoring to achieve
Does not exist
Each diamond is unique in their own ways
Why compare different individuals
when,
everyone makes mistakes,
shines in their own colors and gloss
Find inspirations
rather than pinpointing what you lack
For they have something you don't
Vice versa

till she flies again

The trick of never failing

There are things in life that you loved doing, but slowly, they turned into routines. You feel numb. You do them because you want to get that good grade, paycheck, or others' recognition. As a result, you lost that passion you once have. Before you know it, that once passionate teenager turned into a robotic figure who is only here because they need to be.

I was invited to a philosophy talk once, and it changed my perspective of things. I didn't expect much from this talk before going, but little did I know that I would've learned something that I carry around with me everywhere now.

The speaker said there are two types of actions in the world— transitive and immanent.

Transitive actions are things you do because you want to get to the result, for example, building a house— the action of building the house is intended to get the result of a beautiful home; or, commuting to work, because you want to arrive at the office. The action itself is not the finishing point, the result is. That's why in the process of doing it, the only thing you see is reaching the end of this action. This action is only successful when you've reached the final goal. Because if you gave up building the house halfway, you'd not get that house you wanted; if you got off the bus on your way to work, you wouldn't arrive at the office in time. Transitive actions are usually the things you are required to do.

Then, there are immanent actions, which are actions that achieve their purpose already while doing them, like, thinking and loving. The result exists within the action. To put into an example, reading— when you read, you are enjoying its process, so the activity by itself is already successful; when you listen to music, you are fulfilling your motive by enjoying the music. You are not listening to it because you want to reach somewhere, you do it because you like it. Immanent actions are always successful because when you do it, you already get the goal.

Something clicked in my mind. If I changed my perspective, would every action be successful?

If you learn to enjoy the process of building a house, regardless of whether you finish it or not, you got the experience of constructing it; taking a bus can be enjoyable too if you look out of the window, observe the world and appreciate the process.

It's like the cheesy saying, "do what you love and you will never work a day." But this time, it's explained to me in such a systematic way.

Of course, this is not a switch. It's impossible for me to turn every action into immanent. But this talk has always been a reminder for me. When things get hard, I try to change my perspective and enjoy the process as it is. It makes tough times so much more tolerable.

Chasing after something you don't have

Everything always seems more beautiful when you don't have it. Once you seized it, you might get the satisfaction you'd wanted for a short period. But after a while, whether you notice it or not, you might start taking it for granted and look for the next thing to chase after. It's a never-ending cycle.

That latest phone model you wanted worth you cutting your daily cost short for. You bought it, felt good about yourself, and flaunted it like it's part of your identity. Until something better came out and you were no longer attached to it.

That dream job you'd worked your ass off for five years to get. You went through rounds and rounds of interviews until you finally earned it. Every day, you looked forward to new challenges going to work, until one day you got exhausted because it's not exciting to you anymore.

If there's something you want so desperately right now, remember this feeling, how much you want it. Then, someday when you get it, recall how it felt like when you wanted it so, so badly. Give it to your older self as a gift and thank yourself for the effort you paid to get here.

And when you're ready, put it down, and do it all over again.

till she flies again

Being a 23

The early 20s is a weird period. You either feel too young or too old.

A fresh graduate who was a senior in college is thrown into this adult world. Just when you thought you've completed your education and are finally ready to put your knowledge into practice, you realize just how much there is to learn. From a senior student to a junior employee, we're starting it from the beginning all over again.

Being a newbie in a company, you feel so young. "How old are you?" is a question you avoid answering. You don't want your age to define your capability, but gradually you realize that your age does reflect something. You find yourself struggling with the work you have to deal with for the first time. You self-doubt sometimes; you compare yourself to others. "Man, they are just so good at it." You wish you can fast-forward time to the day when you are just as good as them. Unfortunately, it's a learning process with no shortcut.

Paradoxically, you feel old. Looking at high school students join university camps and talk about schoolwork makes you feel like it's been forever since you were in the same shoes. You just kickstarted adulthood, but you're already 23. That feels so far from being a 16, but so close to being a 30, you told yourself. There are a million things to be taken care of, things that you didn't have to worry about when you were a student because all you had to do was to tackle the homework and exams that were put in front of you. You thought you wouldn't feel as lost when you are secured with a job. It's quite the opposite. You have the freedom to make decisions for yourself and yet you have no idea where to start.

You don't know how to position yourself sometimes, but the most important thing is that you know what you have right now is golden because you're in the process of transitioning to someone you desire to be. Of course, it takes time, but well, you have time. And if circumstances allow it, you could make bold decisions, with minimum risks, to completely turn your life around.

This is a note to self.

Belief or believe

Naive girl in a sheep dress
Sang to the lullaby of Christ
Five loaves and two fishes
Took a piece with her
There'd be a trophy
Waiting in heaven
As a reward for being good

Is it a tale
Made-believe
Hard for her to tell

Wool got thicker
To a new gown
Explores world's mystery
Forgotten the big piece

Somehow
Shepherd comes back to her field
Felt his absence
Peeked into his presence

Doubtful still
"It's just luck"
Crazy coincidence
"It's the law of attraction"

Navigate to follow
Flies on to wander
Sheep dress still floats
In the sky of wonder

till she flies again

What-ifs

Countless choices are laid out in front of us, but we only get to do one thing at a time. If the moment passed, it might be gone forever. And that's life.

That brings us to the what-ifs.

"What if I'd chosen a different major? What if I decided to take a completely different path instead? Would I have had a different destiny?" We are stuck in this loop of wonders, questions that we'd never get an answer to, because honey, we decided on another path, remember? We tend to romanticize the possibilities because they only live in our imagination. In that ideal world, everything seems so perfect and stress-free. It is the other side of the grass that always looks greener than it really is.

What-if is just an escape, an excuse for myself to imagine a life beyond what I have now. It's to fantasize the chances I could've taken, which are too many to even start counting. Nothing productive comes out of it because we could never turn back time and do it again.

Whenever I find myself pondering them again, I remind myself that I've already accomplished many what-ifs in life.

If I didn't choose English as my University major, I probably wouldn't have explored my interests in literary work further; if I didn't make the move to relocate to a different country, I wouldn't meet all these people that inspired me. As much as I didn't do many "what-ifs" in life, I made numerous decisions that landed me where I am today. And I wouldn't give up all these paths that I've taken for all the "what-ifs." That's all it matters, right?

Sometimes though, things are better left being just a what-if. I've heard stories of people dreaming about traveling to a city only to have their dreams crushed after visiting, because the place was not what they anticipated it'd be. It seems too perfect in their imagination. Don't get me wrong, I'm not saying that they shouldn't have gone. I mean that if they hadn't gone, they shouldn't have beaten themselves up over it.

Similarly, I was dying to go to this concert, but it was held on the other side of the world, worse yet, during my exam period. It's a bit indulgent to be traveling all the way for a concert, but I did have a think because it's a once-in-a-lifetime experience. Ultimately, I thought to myself that it's too big of a sacrifice on my part. It'd be a dream come true to be there in person, but after weighing out all the factors, I was not sure if it'd be worth the price. I learned to be okay with the what-if this time. It looked so dreamy in my head—I'd be jumping in the crowd with a bunch of strangers, lifting my hands, reaching for the colorful confetti flying around the stadium, appreciating how great it is to be alive. Perhaps sometimes it's okay for it to only live in our heads. Reality rarely lives up to our expectations anyway. At least that's the mindset to make myself feel better.

There is a reason we made the decision the way we did. When time passes, we might look back and think otherwise. We might start wondering what good could've come out of it if we had just done it differently. But it's all up in the air. We haven't lived it to prove it.

I know eventually, we'd still daydream about the what-ifs. But I hope that we'd be able to tell ourselves that what's been done can't be changed, and more importantly, there is still time to manifest those wonders.

till she flies again

Live like a time-traveler

Think of yourself as a time-traveler
Who came back in time
From 30 years in the future

What would you have done differently?

Think of this as a second chance
Of being that naive self again
Young, wild and free

Would you have changed anything?

This time
You are going to make this right
This time
You are not going to let your future self down

till she flies again

Memento mori

In the culture I was brought up in, it's taboo to talk about death. But stories from friends, family or even news headlines continue to remind me just how inevitable this stage of life is, regardless of whether we want to talk about it or not.

Death seems very far from us until something unexpected happened. You don't know how to react because you didn't even think about the possibility of it happening. That makes me wonder, when is a time when people start thinking about death? After a diagnosis of a deadly cancer? When they reach a certain age?

At the end of the day, no one could truly expect it. Tomorrow is not promised.

This idea scares me a lot— someone getting wiped out from this world without notice and not getting a chance to say their last words. They just went "poof," disappeared from this world, and only exist in people's memories.

One of my friends has a "Memento Mori" tattoo on her arm. I witnessed her getting it in the tattoo shop which was a surreal experience. This phrase translates to "remember you will die" in Latin. It seems such a dark message to be tattooed on one's arm, but she explained to me that it's a reminder to her not to worry too much about the present. These things don't last forever.

Death is too depressing to be thinking about all the time, but it's a prompt of the pure existence we equally have in this world. Not necessarily in the way of the cliché "YOLO" mentality, but it's a reminder to ourselves what truly matters in life. When you are too caught up with whatever is in front of you, you might only focus on those things, whether they are your group projects, workplace politics, or just anything temporary that distracts you from your "eternity".

Maybe we should start living like we are dying. Because let's face it, we all are.

Start making plans now instead of later. At least, that's what I told myself when I started having the idea of publishing a book. Because I know that if I died tomorrow, that'd be something I'd regret not doing. If I start implementing this state of mind in my life, perhaps I'd be more motivated to make the best of what I have right now.

It is definitely easier said than done. But once in a while, I zone out of my current life and look at it from a bigger picture; what my future self would say, would be what I'll try doing today.

till she flies again

till she flies again

A record of gratitude

Giving thanks

In the process of writing, I was sometimes distracted by overthinking about what I should write and what I should leave to myself. Because this book will be published publicly after all. It's my first time doing anything like this so I wanted to make sure I'm doing it right.

Eventually I've figured that it'd only hinder me from expressing my thoughts. If I cared too much about what others think, this book would be written for the perception of others and not myself. So I decided to let it go, at least try to.

I'm a nostalgic person and words to me are like a memory capsule. It's a way for me to capture those moments in a jar and open it from time to time. I strive to be able to write about my memories and feelings in the most precise way possible. So when I read them, I could relive those moments. It does take courage for me to share these writings because I pulled my heart out writing them. I hope to make people feel something. If my words could convey that feeling just half of what it is like, I'd be contented.

I didn't share my writing habits with many people because I wasn't ready to show others my work. It's quite a vulnerable side of me I'd say. I started putting my writings publicly for mostly strangers and close friends to read, to a point where I knew this'd only take me so far. I need to be committed and try something new if I want to keep stepping up my game.

Writing this book, I got to explore myself further and push my limits. I'm really thankful for my supportive friends and family who believed in me way before the day I told them this idea. You know who you are. I'd like to take the time to just give a shout-out to a few people here. They are important to me in the journey of this book, and of course the journey of this ride. Thank you, Allison, Michaela, Oscar, Zeke, JP, Andrea, Riddhi, Meroo, and of course my beautiful parents and my sister Winna. The list can go on forever but I shall thank you in real life personally.

I knew I had to do it because it felt right. And I'm so glad I took this step. I hope it's the first to many more.

Lastly, thank YOU for reading. You might know me personally, you might not. But it doesn't matter because you reading this far already means you're a real one.

I hope this book is something you'd reach for once in a while when you feel sentimental. I hope it brings out different perspectives for you and resonates with you in some ways. This is all I want to do with this book really.

Take care, and let's all figure out this thing called life.

Until next time,
Angel

till she flies again

till she flies again

*If you want to share your thoughts,
feel free to reach me via lifeiscarousel@gmail.com.*

Printed in Great Britain
by Amazon